T0145133

Red Bay Before 1956 | Copyright Charles Wheatley

the story of

RED BAY
east end

Red Bay 2019 | Compliments of Mangoman Photography

Charles Wheatley OBE, PhD | Tortola, British Virgin Islands

The Story of Red Bay, East End

Copyright © 2020 Charles H. Wheatley, OBE, PhD.

All rights reserved. No part of this book may be used or reproduced by any means, graphic, electronic, or mechanical, including photocopying, recording, taping or by any information storage retrieval system without the written permission of the author except in the case of brief quotations embodied in critical articles and reviews.

The views expressed in this work are solely those of the author and do not necessarily reflect the views of the publisher, and the publisher hereby disclaims any responsibility for them

iUniverse books may be ordered through booksellers or by contacting:

iUniverse
1663 Liberty Drive
Bloomington, IN 47403
www.iuniverse.com
1-800-Authors (1-800-288-4677)

Because of the dynamic nature of the internet, any web addresses or links contained in this book may have changed since publication and may no longer be valid. The views expressed in this work are solely those of the author and do not necessarily reflect the views of the publisher, and the publisher hereby disclaims any responsibility for them.

Any people depicted in stock imagery provided by Getty Images are models, and such images are being used for illustrative purposes only.
Certain stock imagery © Getty Images.

Interior Image Credit: Reuben Vanterpool, Dean Greenaway , Mango man, Sam Davies

ISBN: 978-1-5320-9476-7 (sc)
ISBN: 978-1-5320-9478-1 (hc)
ISBN: 978-1-5320-9477-4 (e)

Library of Congress Control Number: 2020915120

Print information available on the last page.

iUniverse rev. date: 08/17/2020

Contents

Acknowledgements

I acknowledge with gratitude the contributions of my deceased parents, Alturo and Marie T. Durante-Wheatley. They shared the stories of their lives with me, and those stories are reflected in this publication in many ways. I cannot forget the impact of my deceased paternal grandparents, Charles and Cornelia Wheatley, as they nurtured my curiosity as a young boy with the stories of their lives. Many times I felt like giving up this project, but my wife, Jennie N. Smith-Wheatley, was always there to encourage and support me in moving forward. My three sons, Ludwis, Lloyd, and Leon, supported me in various ways as I developed this project, and I thank them for their contributions. My siblings, Eva, William, Edris, Cecelia, Oraldo, Sonia, Walterdin, Lucita, and Edgar, always responded to my appeals for help, and I thank them. I must mention my grandchildren, Jenelle, Daniele, Arianna, and Amarie; my great-grandchildren, Carter, Leah Marie, and Cale Monet; my special niece, Joy, for their efforts in inspiring me to keep young at heart. Special thanks to Reuben Vanterpool for the illustrations, Dean Greenaway for the images which he provided, and Junior Daniel for images and technical support in the layout of the book.

This book is
dedicated to
the children and young people
in the
British Virgin Islands

Introduction

As I travel along Red Bay daily, I lament the changes that have taken place. Red Bay has lost almost all of its original identity. The recent reclamation works which have taken place changed the Red Bay that was known to the people of East End. As I reflect on the transformation that has taken place, I realize that my grandchildren and all their peers will see only the twenty-first-century reclaimed Red Bay. The twentieth-century Red Bay exists only in the minds of those whose life journeys put them in contact with it.

I have tried to capture the spirit of the activities which occurred in Red Bay on a daily, weekly, monthly, and annual basis. Berthing boats was a daily activity, swimming was mostly a weekly activity, departing by boat from the jetty for St Croix was a monthly activity, visits by sailors from Her Majesty's ships anchored in Drake Channel were an annual activity. Activities like the operation of a shark company in the late 1920s were one-time activities.

Red Bay was the cradle of the economy of East End. I am sure some curious minds would enquire as to why the bay is named Red Bay. Indeed, what is red about Red Bay? Before the construction of Blackburn Highway, which passes along Red Bay, was completed in 1956, Red Bay was strewn with red rocks. The rocks were the type like the large red rocks which are presently situated in the harbour to the south of the bay.

The houses adjacent to Red Bay are built on an outcrop of those red rocks which jutted out into

Red Rocks in the Harbour
Courtesy of Mangoman Photography

the sea before the days of motorable road. The outcrop is still there behind the houses, and if you look carefully you will see those rugged rocks pointing to the sky. The bay got its name from these rocks. When Blackburn Highway was being constructed, the stones on the shore were broken up and used for the construction of the road. The few small rocks that remained in the bay were buried in the sand of the reclaimed land. Today there are no red rocks along the bay, but the name Red Bay remains. I hope that the red rocks in the harbour will not be destroyed by people's developments but will be a permanent example of the rocks which give their colour to the name of Red Bay.

In this publication, I hope to provide a record for future generations to be able to compare the life of Red Bay as they experience it with the life of Red Bay many decades ago. Many of the senior citizens of East End remember their first experience walking on the wharf at Red Bay. The wharf was built on wooden piles driven into the sand and fastened together by strong wooden beams to form a platform. The piles and the beams were made of hard greenheart wood which would last a very long time. Planks, usually two inches thick and about ten inches wide, were nailed to the frame of this platform, with a space of one to two inches between each plank. The sea under the planks was visible through these spaces. Young children were always scared to walk from one plank to the other on their first journey to the wharf. They were afraid of falling through the spaces. Travelling across these planks for the first time was almost a rite of passage.

I hope that as you read this book, you feel a part of Red Bay. I hope that you will be hungry for more of the history of the British Virgin Islands and that you will record your life's journey for future generations.

Chapter 1

Red Bay Before 1956

The bay got its name from the end of an outcrop of metamorphic rocks which jutted into the middle of the bay. The outcrop extended from the hill to the north of the bay. To the south of the bay across the harbour, another outcrop of large red rocks can be seen.

These rocks are called Red Rock, a well-established marine point of reference for sailors. Southwest of Red Rock is Red Shoal, a submerged outcrop of red rocks on which corals

Red Bay jetty.
Copyright Charles Wheatley.

have grown. Red Shoal was a hazard to sailors before the advent of marine harbour lights. Many boats ran aground on it.

The magic names "Red Bay", "Red Rock", and "Red Shoal" are names that not only have economic and social significance for the people of East End, Fat Hogs Bay, and Long Look, but also have been infused in the culture of the area. Red Bay has been a reference point in giving directions to travellers in the village. The red rocks of Red Bay extended eastward to what was known as "Muggy Rock". These rocks formed a roadside park where people gathered to relax in the evenings after work and on weekends. It was also a centre for discussing the current events of the week. This was a common means of sharing information in an age without radio, telephone, or television.

Before I discuss the economic and social significance of Red Bay in the life of the East End community, I would like you to imagine what the pristine, innocent bay looked like

before humans interrupted its natural beauty and defaced its appearance. Before the onslaught of dynamite and bulldozers carved out Blackburne's Motorway in 1956, the area where the gas station and Red Rock Restaurant stand in 2019 cradled the rugged outcrop of red rocks which I mentioned earlier.

Red Bay jetty.
Copyright Charles Wheatley.

The whole area was a small cliff in which the inhabitants dug out a path wide enough to accommodate pedestrians and horse riding. It was a short geometric dance to wind through these rocks. It was the place where travellers could wash their feet in the clear-crystal waters of the Caribbean Sea. One only had to sit on a rock and idly stroke the ripples of the water with one's feet. It was soothing and medicinal to weary feet. If your shirt lost a button, you could pick a thorn from the nearby cactus hedge growing among the rocks and fasten the shirt together. These thorns were referred to by the children of the day as "golden pins". The thorns were yellow like gold and could range from three-fourths of an inch to one and a half inches long.

It was a very tranquil and romantic experience to sit and watch the tiny waves beat against the rocks, circle around them, and reshuffle the pockets of white sand surrounding the rocks. There were several pools of water, some big enough for bathing. The inside of one of these pools was like a modern Jacuzzi when the waves rolled in and out and the current encircled the rocks. Such a bath had to be carefully monitored because a lurking conger eel under the rocks could attack the feet and inflict dangerous bites on swimmers. Another hazard was the black sea egg (sea urchin—Echinoidea), which could ruin the pleasure of a swimmer's bath if he or she happened to step on one. The spines, called "needles", would penetrate one's flesh, and one's pleasure would immediately turn into pain which could last for several days.

Sea urchins.
Courtesy of Dean Greenaway.

Another teenage activity which took place on the rocks was fishing. Many young boys learned the art of fishing with a hook at the end of a fishing line. One had to learn the art of fixing the bait on the hook and the skills of throwing the line and pulling the catch to the shore without losing it.

On the immediate eastern side of the rocks was the government-built jetty which connected East End with other parts of Tortola and the other islands in the Virgin Islands. It also connected this part of Tortola with the US Virgin Islands and other Caribbean Islands. East of the jetty, the bay changed into a gravel shoreline with a darker seabed. In this area, the fishermen dried and mended their fishing nets, repaired and made their fish traps, and put their boats in dry dock to clean them. In the next chapter, we will see Red Bay as a fish market.

Fishing with a line at Red Rock.
Courtesy of Dean Greenaway.

Chapter 2

Selling Fish at Red Bay

The statement "The seine boat is out" refers to fishermen who went to other locations to catch fish with a long net called a seine; the boat carrying the seine was called the seine boat. This boat was built specially to accommodate the long net. The eyes of all the villagers would eagerly watch to see the boat coming home along Ella Reef. This is the reef that joins the red rocks in the harbour to Ella Point. The ears of everyone would be listening attentively to hear the first call of the conch shell. Suddenly the call would come ringing through the air, and people everywhere would cry out, "The seine boat round!" That meant the men had caught fish. The boat would pass Red Rock and head for Red Bay. Someone from almost every household would head to the jetty at Red Bay. Soon the jetty would be crowded, the boat would be berthed alongside the jetty, and the sale of fish would begin. If the catch was a small one, each customer would be sold a limited amount of fish to enable everyone to get some fish. This would happen several times a week during the season when the cavalli, hardnose fish, yellow-tail, and bonitos were near to the land. The fish were lured to the land by the tiny fish fry upon which they fed.

When the catch was a bountiful one and there were more fish than could be sold at Red Bay, the boat would then travel to another jetty in Fat Hog's Bay to sell fish. Villagers from Fat Hog's Bay, Long Look, and Old Plantation would go to that jetty to purchase fish.

If the fish were caught late in the afternoon, they would be kept in the nets near the shore until the following morning, when the catch would be taken to market at East End, Road Town, or Cane Garden Bay. The fishermen called this method of holding the fish for market "kraal out". Other times they placed their fish in a corral—an enclosure with rocks near the shore where the fish could swim in the flowing water.

Selling fish at Red Bay.
Copyright Charles Wheatley.

If the market was filled with fish and the sale was small, the fishermen would "corn"—that is, preserve their fish with salt. The villagers would refer to the salted fish as corned fish. This was before the days of refrigeration. The sale of corned fish was a common feature of life in the mid-twentieth century. These fishermen prepared a fish to be salted by cutting it open along the back from head to tail. All the intestines would be removed and the flesh cut into thin slices about an inch wide. The salt was then packed in the crevices between the slices to preserve the fish. The slices were then dried and taken to market. Corned fish is similar to the salt fish which we import from North America. Sometimes the fishermen may have many hundred pounds of corned fish and may take it to another market in St Thomas, or St Croix in the US Virgin Islands. Today the fish can be frozen and sold over periods of weeks or longer.

Fish traps at Red Bay dock.
Courtesy of Dean Greenaway.

There was another type of fisherman who fished with fish traps called "fish pots". They selected various fishing grounds, which they called banks, to set their traps. After they collected the catch from their traps, they too would head for Red Bay, where the sale would take place. Before the construction of Blackburn Highway, there were a number of small bays along the coast where fish was sold. Two of these bays are Joe Rhymers Bay and James Young. Wherever the fish was landed, that was where the sale usually took place. There were a few exceptions when the fishermen would ask the customers to come to their homes, where the sale would take place.

Selling fish at home.
Courtesy of Reuben Vanterpool.

Today Red Bay is still the only fishing port in East End, but in a different way. The new reclamation of land in the bay will accommodate a modern facility for fishermen. The development will facilitate berthing facilities as well as facilities for launching boats and pulling boats out of the sea for cleaning and repair work. There will also be parking accommodation. We can refer to these developments as the "New Red Bay".

Chapter 3

Red Bay: East End Port

The Tortola boat was the most common and most important means of sea transport to the US Virgin Islands (St Thomas, St Croix, and St John) and other Caribbean islands, including the Dominican Republic, Trinidad, Antigua, St Kitts, Saint-Barthélemy (St Barts), and St Martin. Those boats transported agricultural produce, sea produce, and products from cottage industries to these islands for sale. The products which were exported included vegetables, fruits, charcoal, fish, salt, straw bags, straw hats, and crocheted items. The boats would leave Red Bay jetty with these exports and return with imports. The imports included building materials, food, and clothing. Sometimes those boats also carried passengers to accompany their exports. When these boats returned, Red Bay was a busy sight, with persons collecting and taking away packages and other hardware imports. Of course they returned with money from the sale of their produce. Those persons who sent exports via the captain or the sailors would wait eagerly to learn if their produce had been sold and to collect their money. The following is a list of boats that took part in that trade.

Passengers at Red Bay.
Copyright Charles Wheatley.

Owners	Names of Boats
Claremond Davies	the *Una*
Claremond Davies	the *Fairwind*
and Alvanley Frett	the *Friendship*
	the *Beauty*
	the *Wasp*
Claremond Davies, Caris Penn, and Adolphus Penn	the *Delma*
Alvanley Frett and Adolphus Penn	the *Liberty*
Caris Penn, Oliver Penn, and Melvin Penn	the *Adella*
Charles E. Penn	the *Briton I*
	the *Dearie*
	May Rose
	Secret
Alvanley Frett	the *Linden*
	the *Spirit of Tortola*
Edward Frett	the *Syria*
	the *Safety*
Edward Frett and	the *Parham Town*
Maxwell Lettsome	the *Darling*
Edward Frett, Clement Frett, and Austin Frett	the *Eden*
Edward Frett and Alvanley Frett	the *Dauntless*
Milton Thomas	the *Ruby*
	the *Lily*
	the *Ivy*
Milton Thomas and	the *Caution*
Archibald Smith	the *Tinkerbell*
Fritz Penn	the *Paloma Bird*
	Briton II
	the *Sea Queen*
	Morning Star
Richard Penn	the *Darling*
Osmond Penn	*Energy*
	Social

Obel Penn	the *Eastern Cross*
Wilfred Penn	the *Briton*
	the *Lady Iris*
Wilfred Penn and Adolphus Penn	the *Excelsis*
Wilfred Penn and Richard Frett	the *Concord*
Reynold Osmond Davies	the *Review*
	the *Herald*
	the *Heron*
	the *Boney*
	the *White Squall*
	the *Youth Instructor*
Haldane Davies	the *Lady D*
	the *Jet*
Isaac Thomas	the *Alpha*
Herman Thomas	the *Ventura*
	the *Dawson*
	the *Effort*
	the *Surprise*
Charles G. Wheatley	the *Dinah*
	the *Ida*
Emile Wheatley	the *Breeze*
	the *Lily*
Joseph Smith	the *Lady Smith*
	the *Daisy*
Joseph Smith, Warren Smith, and Landsdell Potter	the *Marilyn G*
	the *Weapon*
Dennis Potter	*Santa Lou*
Milford Chalwell	*Octavia C*
	Octavia C II
Ebert Lettsome	the *Lower Light*
Oswald Frett	the *Butting Ram*

Red Bay Wharf.
Courtesy of Dean Greenaway.

Red Bay Wharf.
Copyright Charles Wheatley.

Chapter 4

Red Bay: Passenger Jetty

On any given Saturday morning, all eyes would be turned towards the haulover—the passage of water between Buck Island and Witches Brew point. There one could see the boats travelling east and west. Eyes would be looking for the motorboat coming from Road Town to collect passengers and take them back to Road Town. Some of the motorboats which transported people were the *Lady Kate*, owned by the government; and other privately owned boats, such as the *Saucy Lou*, *Four Friends*, *Islander*, *St George*, the *Neptune*, and the *Joan of Arc*. As soon as the motorboat was in sight, everyone would make haste to get to Red Bay in time to embark on the motorboat when it docked alongside the jetty.

Passengers travelling through Red Bay.
Copyright Charles Wheatley.

Passengers travelled to Road Town to visit friends, sell produce, and visit the doctor. Sometimes one person would go for all three reasons and return in the afternoon on the same motorboat. On a few occasions one might travel on one motorboat and return on another. These motorboats usually left Road Town promptly at 2 p.m.

Red Bay was an exciting place to be when the motorboat was taking the passengers to Road Town, but it was even more exciting when the boat returned. The luggage was placed on the jetty, and all the passengers disembarked and collected it. Sometimes pieces of luggage were misplaced and taken away by the wrong person, and it would take hours or perhaps a day or two before they would be returned to their owners.

The motorboats also made midweek trips to St Thomas, US Virgin Islands, taking passengers on one day and returning the following day. People travelled to St Thomas to look for employment as well as to sell produce from cottage industries, such as hats and bags made from straw, crocheted items, and knitted work. If the motorboat left on Tuesday morning, it would return on Wednesday afternoon. The return of the motorboat from St Thomas brought as much or more excitement as the return of the motorboat from Road Town on a Saturday afternoon. All those persons who expected relatives to return home would hasten to Red Bay to meet them. Girls and women were interested in people visiting from New York, what they were wearing, and how their hair looked, to determine style and fashion.

Chapter 5

Red Bay and the Methodist Church

Before the advent of motorable roads on Tortola, people travelled from one village to another on Sunday mornings to attend the Methodist church harvest celebrations in the afternoon. Some people travelled by horse, while others walked. Persons from faraway villages travelled by motorboats—those same motorboats that took them to Road Town on Saturday or to St Thomas during the week. These motorboats made a special trip to Red Bay on Sunday mornings to take passengers to Cane Garden Bay; Carrot Bay; West End; Jost Van Dyke; or the Valley, Virgin Gorda, to attend these harvest celebrations. They were really excursion trips for pleasure rather than attending church activities.

In most villages it was a minifestival, and the festive celebrations would be going at the same time the church celebrations were taking place. People would set up small booths along the roadside as they do today to sell food, drinks, ground provisions, and any other saleable goods, such as preserved fruits. The consumption of alcoholic beverages was not forbidden, so the men drank large quantities and sometimes became intoxicated.

The motorboat returned in the afternoon. The scene was usually different from the departing scene in the morning. There would be a lot of merriment on the boat as many of the intoxicated men sang and shouted for joy. Other passengers would rejoice because they'd had a very enjoyable church experience. Best of all, many returned with all kinds of goods which they'd purchased from the vendors.

This was a cultural experience, as it afforded people the opportunity to exchange views on various subjects. Women exchanged recipes, men exchanged agricultural techniques, and they all learned something more about the geography of the village they were visiting and the struggles of the people to survive. New friendships developed, and old acquaintances were renewed. This was one of the simple ways that brought people together and helped in building national pride.

Red Rocks in the harbour.
Courtesy of Mangoman Photography.

Chapter 6

Red Bay and Her Majesty's Ships

During the late 1940s and early 1950s, the British Virgin Islands was one of the places where Her Majesty's training ships would visit so that the sailors could get a rest from their training exercises. These ships usually anchored in Sir Francis Drake Channel between Beef Island and Ginger Island. The sailors would make many visits to East End, Tortola, and Beef Island. Red Bay was the famous place for disembarking in East End. When the sailors were in the village, the people of the village would be very alert and watchful for clashes between the sailors and the villagers. Sometimes when the sailors were intoxicated, they would clash with some of the inhabitants. These skirmishes were short-lived most of the time. One noted incident was an attack on a Polish resident on Beef Island. His name was Wagner, and the altercation ended in punishment for the sailors and compensation for the damages inflicted on Wagner's body.

Sometimes when the sailors landed at Red Bay, they came to entertain the community. Two forms of entertainment were cricket matches and musical concerts. In those days, cricket was the main sport in the British Virgin Islands, and there were some excellent cricketers in the territory. Thus they were very happy and willing to play against the sailors. Such a game would attract the whole village, and everyone would be shouting and cheering for the local team. After the game was over, everyone mixed and mingled for refreshments. The other form of entertainment was musical concerts. The sailors would bring the ship's band to East End Methodist Church and would perform for the public. They were free concerts, and they were usually well attended.

Red Bay, 1956.
Copyright Charles Wheatley.

Chapter 7

The Village Beach

Saturdays and holidays were the days when most boys had free time. Boys did limited domestic work and spent most of their free time hiking, fishing, swimming, sailing, punting, sculling, and rowing around the East End harbour. Red Bay was one of the famous places where these boys gathered to swim. There were those who could not swim, but they would wade out into the sea to a depth they were comfortable with. There they enjoyed themselves as they struggled to learn to swim. They usually drank a lot of seawater as they struggled to keep afloat.

Those who could swim would jump off the end of the jetty as one might jump from a diving board into a swimming pool. They performed all kinds of movements: diving, somersaulting, swimming on the back, swimming the breaststroke, and playing ball games. Sometimes they competed in teams to show their skills and knowledge of water sports. During school holiday, these activities were repeated daily, and not only on the weekend.

Sometimes members from the group of nonswimmers received swimming instruction from members of the groups of swimmers. It was on occasions like these that older siblings taught their younger siblings to swim and dive.

Today no one swims in the water at Red Bay or anywhere along the shore from East End to Fat Hog's Bay. The water is polluted with residue from the paint on yachts and other boats, sewage from the land, and debris carried into the sea by running water from rainfall on the land.

Swimming at Red Bay, 1956.
Copyright Charles Wheatley.

The residents who graduated from these experiences have fond
memories of those happy days—those good old days.

Chapter 8

The Bigelows of Guana Island

On Saturday afternoons, if one listened carefully, one could hear the noise from the engine of a little service boat named the *Pelican*. It was the ferryboat that connected Guana Island and Tortola. Guana Island is situated north of the eastern end of Tortola. (See the map of the British Virgin Islands on page 29.) It was owned by the Bigelows, and they transported their workers on this little motorboat. The trips to Red Bay were also shopping tours. The crew on this little boat purchased large quantities of goods from the village merchants and took them back to Guana Island. All these activities took place in East End, Tortola, during the 1940s and 1950s.

On Saturday the Bigelow family would make the trip to Tortola to do the shopping and especially to purchase fresh meat from the local butchers. Very often the butchers would sell them the choicest cuts, and the local customers were unhappy about this. These feelings did not create any bad relations between the black population and the Bigelows, who were Caucasians. To the contrary, the local population embraced them because they were very friendly. They mixed with the black population quite easily and respected the black people. The Bigelows were very fond of some local shrubs which they cooked in the same style as we cook spinach today. These shrubs were edible, but the local population fed their pigs with them. This in no way was degrading to the Bigelows. It was a cultural pattern in the community which was passed down from one generation to another. The same attitude was displayed about the papaya. The local people fed the pigs with the papaya fruit and seldom ate it. Today that cultural behaviour has changed; papaya is now a prized fruit.

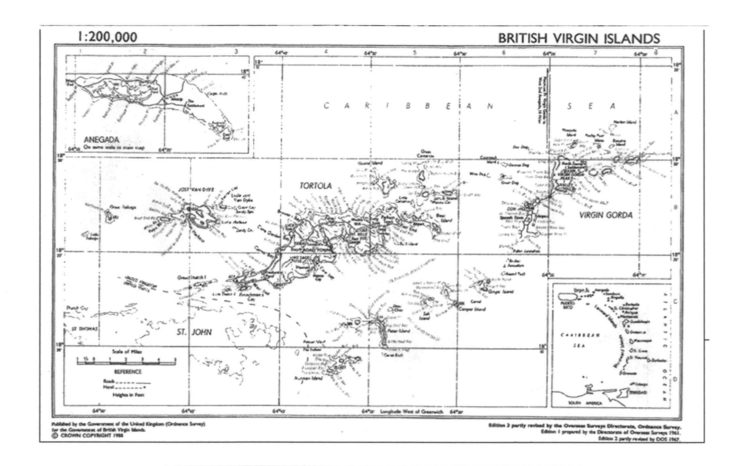

Map of the British Virgin Islands, Courtesy of
Survey Department, British Virgin Islands.

Many housewives looked forward to the arrival of the *Pelican* on Saturday in particular. Guana Island was famous for the palm tree known locally as the broom tyre tree. The leaves from this plant, when cut young, were used by the ladies for making hats and bags. This was part of a straw cottage industry which was common in East End. The more mature leaves were cut by the men and woven into brooms. These brooms were very strong, and they swept the floor clean. When the *Pelican* came from Guana Island, the crew brought bundles of the young leaves for sale and dozens of brooms also for sale. These products were sold at Red Bay to the housewives. Mr Walter Penn was a long-standing employee of the Bigelows on Guana Island and was one of the captains of the *Pelican*. He was very famous for making these brooms. No one could make a broom like him, and the housewives always purchased his brooms before buying those of any other maker of brooms.

Red Bay from the sky.
Courtesy of Mangoman Photography.

Chapter 9

The Shark Company

A shark company was started at Red Bay in 1928 by William Young of Honolulu and John Bleau of Dominica. The company's headquarters was established on land owned by Mr John Smith, on the site where the Iris Penn-Smith Clinic now stands. They established their homes on the little hill adjacent to Red Bay. Before the company was established at Red Bay, a branch was established at Red Hook, St Thomas. Most of the activities took place on land, but some were carried out on a large barge which was anchored in Red Bay. The company also owned a boat named the *Venus*, which transported supplies to and from St Thomas.

The company provided employment for many of the residents of East End—especially men who were fishermen. These fishermen fished for the sharks. They used large galvanized hooks to which they attached the bait—a fish or a piece of meat. The hooks were then attached to ropes, and the ropes would then be attached to floating buoys. Each trap would be placed in the sea unattended until the shark swallowed the bait. The shark would then be pulled into the boat. On some days, the men would catch as many as fifteen sharks; but on other days just one or two were caught.

Mr Obel Penn reported that on one particular day, a fisherman caught a shark which weighed over fifteen hundred pounds. It was so heavy that the scale could not weigh it. This shark was caught to the west of Guana Island and could not be taken in the boat. It was towed into Red Bay.

When the sharks arrived at Red Bay, they were butchered, and the liver was separated from the remainder of the body. The livers were boiled in large iron cauldrons over large fires.

Iron cauldron from shark company. This iron cauldron was given to Mahitabel Smith when the shark company folded in 1934. She was the foster mother of Marie T. Durante-Wheatley, who inherited it and used it for storing water. Charles Wheatley inherited it from his mother, Marie T. Durante-Wheatley. He used it as a decorative garden item until Hurricanes Irma and Maria destroyed the garden in 2017. It will continue to be used for this purpose. Copyright Charles Wheatley.

This process extracted the oil from the liver. When the contents cooled, the oil was skimmed off the water, bottled, and packed for shipment to Red Hook, St Thomas. It was later manufactured for sale.

The company carried out these activities for about five years. In addition to employment the company contributed to the social life of the community. The manager of the company gave assistance to the East End Methodist School and helped some children by giving them books and pencils. He also organized periodic entertainment for the villagers in the form of birthday celebrations and fetes. It was a brief period in the life at Red Bay, but it is a period to be remembered.

The information in this chapter was passed on orally to me by my late mother, Marie T. Durante-Wheatley, who lived on the grounds where the headquarters of the company was erected; the late Iva Varlack, who worked with the company; and the late Obel Penn, who was associated with the company.

Red Bay in the twenty-first century.
Courtesy of Mangoman Photography.

Chapter 10

Twenty-First-Century Red Bay

Today the name "Red Bay" is almost forgotten. Most people, if asked where Red Bay is, would say they do not know. Of course, the red is gone out of Red Bay because the Red Rocks from which the bay's name is derived have either been buried under the sand from reclamation or have been blown up by dynamite for construction purposes. However, viewed from the sea, one can see in the background of the bay an outcrop of those red rocks still projecting into the sky on the top of a small hill. The shore along the bay has given way to reclaimed land. The jetty has gone. Boats now berth at the edge of the concrete breakwater which protects the reclaimed land. The natural beauty of the surrounding area has faded away, as the trees and other features of the land gave way to the construction of buildings. What was once a pristine area for sea bathing, fishing, and nursing small sea creatures is now buried under a fossil fuel station, a marina, and a restaurant.

In addition to the physical changes, one can identify changes in the economic, social, and cultural activities within the area. The area is no longer an area where fishermen market their catch. The means of transportation have changed, and fishermen can take their fish to market by land transportation. The fishermen drive through the villages and sell their fish. Other commodities, such as petrol, diesel, and propane gas, are sold in the area for domestic and commercial purposes. There is a launching pad where boats can be launched into the sea and can be pulled out of the sea for repairs and maintenance.

Social activities in Red Bay are limited to village group discussions which mirror the traditional group discussions held under the great tamarind trees at Joe Rhymers Bay, Parham Town, and James Young and the small coconut grove at Tarris Hill. While a great deal of the discussions are for recreational purposes, discussions on current events in the territory, the region, and the wider world often take place. One may easily say it is an area for familiarization, because individuals there get to know one another and meet visitors from other places.

The area also reflects the changing culture of the British Virgin Islands. The surrounding buildings are no longer built from wood but from blocks, bricks, and concrete. The Tortola boats which once dominated the harbour have given way to yachts and speedboats. This is a radical change. The changes in ownership are also significant. While the local people own the Tortola boats, the yachts, for the most part, are owned by nonnationals. As you will have noted in the earlier parts of this book, Red Bay was a place for recreational activities like swimming, rowing, punting, and sculling small boats around the harbour. Today you can see small boats driven by engines going to and fro, mostly for economic reasons. That is a significant cultural change that has occurred during the last fifty years.

The question we should address is, What are we doing to preserve what we have not destroyed? If we neglect to save our country for future generations of British Virgin Islanders, then our children, grandchildren, great-grandchildren, and beyond will all be strangers in the land of their heritage. The best we can do for them regarding the past ways of life in these islands is to record in print or electronic form what we have experienced and can remember.

I have tried to do this for Red Bay, and I hope whoever reads this book gets a glimpse into what Red Bay was like before 1956 and the changes that have taken place between 1956 and 2019.

Charles H. Wheatley began his career in education as a class teacher in February 1955 in East End Methodist School. He served as a head teacher of North Sound Methodist School, West End Methodist School, Cane Garden Bay Methodist School, East End Methodist School, and Road Town Elementary School. He was also the first local principal of the British Virgin Islands High School, having served in that position for eight years. He then went on to serve as chief education officer for seven years, followed by four years as permanent secretary for the Ministry of Health, Education, and Welfare. He left that position to serve as president of the H. Lavity Stoutt Community College for the next fourteen years. He became president emeritus of this college, which was followed by twelve years as chairman of the Board of Governors.

Wheatley was educated at the Leeward Islands Teachers Training College, the College of Preceptors, Mount Allison University, the University of Toronto, Union Institute and University, Harvard University, Carnegie Mellon University, and the University of Oklahoma. Dr Wheatley was honoured by the University of the West Indies for twenty-five years of service as a local representative of the university and by the Caribbean Examinations Council for fifteen years of service as a member of the council. He has been the local representative of the Royal Schools of Music and has supervised the certification of hundreds of students in music since 1978. He was awarded an OBE medal in 1996 and is the recipient of many awards from churches, service clubs, and other organizations.

Wheatley has written many articles on education and plans to share his experience with generations to come. In this publication, he records the story of Red Bay, East End.

Printed in the United States
By Bookmasters